For the Love of Pink

Written by Nikita Hollins

ISBN # 978-0-998-0933-0-7

Text Copyright 2016

Printed in the USA

nannynikkistory.com

nannynikkistory@gmail.com

The Nanny Nikki Series

This book is dedicated to the tiny humans who are tomorrow's society.
I would like to thank everyone who invested time in me, my project, and my dreams.
This book series is the evidence of the fruits of your labor.
Thank you so very much.
Your continued help and support means more than I can say!

Contributors:

April & Ivan Mbakop
Norma Hollins
Eric "Mosteel" Hollins Sr.
Eric Hollins Jr.
Branislav Gapic

Darrell "Red" Campbell Jr.
Derrick Montgomery
Denise Montgomery
Ricardo Salinas
Nicole Hollins

Terrazia Robinson
Armondo G. Beats
Vladimyr Prokhorenko
Carolyn Daniels
Nikita Hollins

Iman was a little girl who loved the color pink. She loved it on cake, she loved it on pie, she loved it on her clothes, she loved it in the sky!

Everyday Iman dressed in her pink clothes, only used pink paper and a pink pencil in school, and only picked pink flowers to go in her vase on her desk. She NEVER wore black, blue, yellow, green or white. Although she was curious about these colors, she never explored them because she didn't want everyone to think that she did not love pink the best, so she only enjoyed pink.

Imans family and friends wished she would explore other colors. However, No matter how many times people begged her to explore a different color, she preferred pink... On everything! She even asked only to eat pink food...If it wasn't pink, she wouldn't have it.

Her sister Ziza, had enough of the pink! She decided she would help expose Iman to other colors.

One morning, while Iman was sitting on her pink blanket, wearing her favorite pink dress, combing her pink pony's hair, when Ziza came to her with a blue cup of water.

"Iman, would you like some water from my blue cup?"

"Thank you, but I would prefer drinking it from my pink princess cup." stated Iman.

"But it tastes the same in the pink cup as the blue cup doesn't it?" Asked Ziza

"Yes, that is true, But think about this, if it tastes the same in either cup, why not drink it in the pink cup which I prefer? Same water, better cup color!"

"Ok...well, I'll get the pink cup for you." Said Ziza, discouraged.

"Thank you!" smiled Iman.

At lunch, Mama had prepared a pink grapefruit along with green asparagus, orange carrots, and brown meatloaf.

Mama asked "Iman, would you like to try different color foods? It's very yummy today!"

"Yes...So Good" Papa said as he quickly ate one fork full after another.

"Mama, Can I have more carrots please?" Asked Navi and he tried to lick the plate when Mama turned around.

"No thank you Mama, I will just have a pink grapefruit"

Iman smelled the asparagus and looked at Ziza. Her eyes were closed as she chewed her carrots and her faced looked as happy as a dog with a bone! Then she glanced over at her brother Navi, and her baby sister Kali crunching on the asparagus and ooooooooh!! how she loooonged for a bite! Slowly she turned her gaze to Mama, who seemed to be eating in slow motion. She used her knife to cut her meatloaf and as it separated Iman could see all the spices explode out of it in a savory smelling smoke.

Then Mama put her fork in the soft slice of meatloaf and seemingly, slowly bought it to her mouth. As she began to chew, her eyes closed, her head tilted to the side and she let out a moan ever so slightly "Mmmm..." Iman was in agony. Nevertheless, while the smell of the meatloaf and spices invaded her nose and everyone else enjoyed their meal, she ate her pink grapefruit and forced herself to smile.

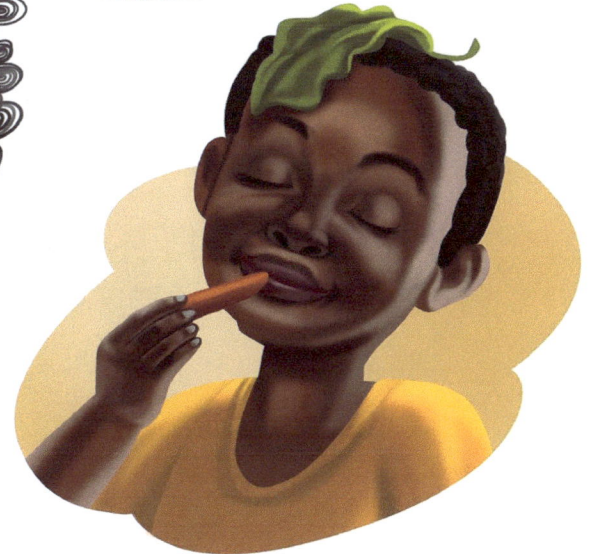

For Dinner, Mama had prepared spaghetti with chunks of the meatloaf from lunch cut up in the tomato sauce.

"Iman, you are really missing out on some good food" Papa said at the dinner table, "You can still love pink and enjoy a wonderful meal. Try a small bit of this and if you still prefer pink food, you can have a grapefruit."

Iman was excited inside but she tried not to show it! The sweet and savory spice flavors had been whirling around her nose all day and FINALLY she was going to have a taste.

But...

She only liked pink. She wanted everyone to know that she only liked pink. Iman felt if she began to show interest in things that were a different color, no one would think she liked pink anymore. So, as much as she wanted to have a heaping plate of spaghetti, in her mind, she knew she could only have a taste and then she would eat her grapefruit...no matter how much her tummy grumbled.

When Mama put the tiny plate with the tiny scoop of spaghetti and one single chunk of meatloaf in front of Iman, she took a deep SNNNNNNIIIFFFFFFFFFFF and as she did, the hairs all over her body danced in excitement and anticipation.

After staring at it for a while, she picked up her fork and quickly glanced up at her family. She was surprised to see everyone staring intensely at her, anticipating her first bite. Ziza just KNEW that this was it, this was the moment where Iman would become excited about things that were a different color than pink, everyone waited excitedly!!

Iman could see the excitement on their faces and as much as she wanted them to be happy with her, she really wanted everyone to know she liked pink the most. So she picked up her fork, and ate the small scoop of spaghetti from her tiny plate. As she chewed, her mouth felt like it was in the middle of a large party! The warm, juicy meatloaf tasted 10 times better than it smelled and she completely understood why Mama said "Mmmmm…" when she ate it. This was so delicious it made her want to break away from the table and sing and dance and bathe in a tub of it!!! Who KNEW food could be so yummy!!!

But don't forget…this is Iman. Once she sets her mind to do something, she will do it… no matter what. So despite the joy she felt, she ate the scoop spaghetti and politely asked for her grapefruit.

"WHHHAT?!" Ziza exclaimed! "Are you serious?! How could you eat that and want to go back to your grapefruit???"

"I just prefer food that is pink" Iman smiled

"Mama! Papa! Something is WRONG WITH THIS CHILD!!! We need to need to take her to a doctor!!! I think her brain in broken!!"

Mama and Papa just smiled at each other and asked,

"Ziza, do you remember when you wore your favorite red socks every day for one year until they had so many holes in them we saw more of your foot than the sock?"

Ziza remembered.

She loved those socks so much! They were perfect and so soft! Mama and Papa had given them to her one year at the Feast and she wanted them to know how much she loved them, so she wore them, and wore them, and wore them! She wore them in bed, at the park, at the beach, in the tub, while running in the grass, walking in the snow, and everywhere else!

...She really loved those socks...but how could she help Iman? Later that day Nanny Nikki came over to help mom. Ziza KNEW Nanny Nikki could come up with a great idea to help...she jumped on her as soon as she came through the door!

"Hi Miss Nikki! I need your help!!"

"Ok, girl! You gotta tackle me to tell me? Or can we have a seat and talk about this? Maybe over tea?

Ziza smiled shy and said "Yes, Miss Nikki"

After Miss Nikki helped mom a little, she and Ziza sat down with their tea and told her all about her dilemma. Miss Nikki thought about it for a minute and said "...Well , what if we show Iman how much we love her by wearing pink? Maybe in time she will see that she can love pink like we love her but enjoy other colors just as we do. What do you think?

"That's Great!!" Ziza exclaimed! Thank you Miss Nikki!!" and she gave her a big hug!

When Ziza woke up the next morning she got to work! She cut, she pasted, she ran, and she hopped!

Iman saw Ziza running about the house and at first, she didn't think much of it, Ziza always had a lot of energy. However, she noticed that Ziza had something pink in her hand each time she saw her.

"What are you doing?" Iman asked Ziza

"You'll see!" Ziza yelled as she raced down the hall past Iman's room.

Ziza told Mama and Papa about her idea to help her sister and Mama and Papa

thought it was a wonderful idea, they even said they would help her! Soon, Iman saw Mama going down the hall to Ziza's room with a large sheet of pink paper and she saw Papa bringing a box filled with pink flowers and butterflies!

Iman knew something was going on...She heard banging and ripping coming from Ziza's room all afternoon!

Iman wondered. "What is she doing?!"

At dinner that night, Ziza wore a pink dress with pink stockings, pink shoes, and pink hair bows in her hair. She requested a pink plate and grapefruit for dinner. When Iman asked Ziza, "Since when do you like pink so much?" Ziza simply replied,

"Since ...today!"

For about a month, Ziza only wore pink. She only ate pink food. She only wrote on pink paper. She only slept on pink sheets.

Iman did not like this. Why was Ziza copying her? Why didn't Ziza were HER favorite color? Why pink? If Ziza only used pink, everyone would know that Ziza loved pink the most...but she didn't! Iman did not like this one bit.

Iman went to Zizas room to ask her to borrow her pink eraser and was surprised to see pink...EVERYWHERE!

The walls were pink, the bed was pink, the desk was pink, even the carpet was pink!! Her entire room was PINK!

Iman cried out in a frustrated tone,"What are you doing?! You don't even like pink! Your favorite color is WHITE! Why didn't you make everything in your room white? Why did you have to choose my favorite color?!"

This was the moment Ziza was waiting for.

"Iman, you are my sister and I love you the most! I want everyone to know how much I love you so I am using your favorite color for everything!"

Iman smiled. She thought that was the sweetest thing! She gave Ziza a hug and told her how special her actions made her feel. Then they sat down together and drew a pretty picture.

While Iman was coloring she started looking around and thinking. She thought it was sweet that Ziza made her world pink because she loved her so much but, she didn't want her to give up all her favorite things just to show her she loved her. She knew Ziza LOVED Mama's meatloaf and chicken and didn't want her to stop loving the color white just because she loved her sister.

So, that night at dinner, Iman told Ziza how she felt. She told her that she could love her AND still enjoy all the things she likes and that she would never think that she loves her any less.

When Iman said this, Ziza, Mama, and Papa smiled.

Ziza responded "You know, as much as you love pink, I would never think you loved it any less just because you used or enjoyed other colors."

Iman looked at Ziza. She looked at Mama. She looked at Papa. Mama said, "Ziza has done all of this for 30 days hoping to show you that no matter what color you enjoy, we love you and will not love you less nor will we think you love pink any less."

Again, Iman looked at Ziza. She looked at Mama. She looked at Papa. Then she looked at the smorgasbord of food in the middle of the dinner table...and BURST INTO TEARS!!

"Thank you!" She said as she ran around the table hugging Ziza, "Thank you! Thank you! Thank you!!"

"I really wanted you all to know that pink was my favorite and if I enjoyed other colors, you would think I didn't like pink anymore! Now I see that regardless of the colors I enjoy, you will always remember that I like pink!"

"Yes Iman, we know you love pink," Papa said, "But now you are free to explore the world of colors out there with no reservations!"

Iman smiled.

"Mama?" Iman called.

"Yes Sweetie?" Mama responded.

"Can I PLEASE have some MEATLOAF!!"

Everyone laughed and gave her a "forks up"! Well...everyone except Navi, he was too busy licking a noodle! Iman ate and ate and ate! Afterwards, her tummy looked like a basketball under her shirt! As she slept that night, she dreamt of all the wonderful tastes and colors she explored at dinner...she couldn't wait for more!

From that day forward, Iman enjoyed every color she could find! She loved how the red flower looked in her vase on her desk and how soft and fluffy her green rug was. She felt calmed as she slept under her blue sheets and on her yellow pillow. She enjoyed colors so much, Mama and Papa allowed her to paint a rainbow, right on her wall!

But remember this was Iman... and Iman loved pink. So every day, she wore a pink butterfly hair bows in her hair because even though she enjoyed other colors, she loved pink the best!

THE END

More from us...

"Original song for the book "Strong Heart"

Download your copy of Strong heart, the original song for this book, a dance to the beat!!

Coloring Book

How would you color the FTLOP book? Let's see your best work! Purchase the coloring book or download coloring pages from the web-site!

Audio Book #FTLOP

Download the audio book and read along with Nanny Nikki and all her voices!

YouTube channel Nanny Nikki Stories

Visit our channel to see our animated versions of our series and other goodies!!

Strong Heart Bracelet

FTLOP Charm Bracelets are special memorabilias that are meant to remind your strong little girl of what makes her special and unique! Carefully choose the charm color that matches the essence of your strong girl!

Bracelet color code:

Blue: Strength and Wisdom

Green: Life and Ambition

Red: Power and Passion

Dark Blue: Loyalty and Trust

Silver: Glamorous and Graceful

Black: Elegance and Mystery

Yellow: Joy and Intellect

Pink: Sweet and Delicate

www.ingramcontent.com/pod-product-compliance
Lightning Source LLC
LaVergne TN
LVHW072108070426
835509LV00002B/79

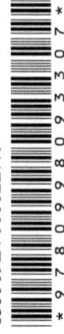